THE BITCOIN
DYSTOPIA
THE PRELUDE

I0504961

DUNSTAN TEO
ALVIN CHIANG

INDIA · SINGAPORE · MALAYSIA

Notion Press

Old No. 38, New No. 6
McNichols Road, Chetpet
Chennai - 600 031

First Published by Notion Press 2019
Copyright © Dunstan Teo and Alvin Chiang 2019
All Rights Reserved.

ISBN 978-1-68466-891-5

Dedication

For Stacey, Aerith and Maia
– Dunstan Teo
For Giselle and Brianna
– Alvin Chiang

Contents

Preface

In a world ruled by fiat currency and credit that mainly serves to further enrich the wealthy elite and the powers that be, Satoshi Nakamoto (be it a single person or a group of people) believed in the decentralisation of the global financial system and created a value transfer system that cannot be manipulated by anyone. Instead of relying on trust (which is the basis of fiat and credit), bitcoin, as the first cryptocurrency, is based on an immutable algorithm. The creator and inventor of bitcoin hopes to usher in a new financial epoch to counter the current problems created by fiat and credit. The layperson will benefit from this ground-breaking system controlled by no one.

We hope to witness a change in the world of finance and credit from its current form to one that relies on debit where one can only spend what they have and not falsely create value by taking value away from those who already hold promissory notes. Value can be robbed in an instant when someone who is responsible for debt becomes unaccountable and takes from others. You, the reader, are the reason why we believe in working towards a better future.

Except for the first and last two chapters, the information gathered for this book can all be found in the public domain. Yet, on their own, they are separate and unconnected.

The intention of writing this book is to piece together seemingly distinct developments in the world of bitcoin, cryptocurrency and the wider global financial system. The objective is to paint a more holistic picture by connecting the dots. We will then be able to better understand the puzzling and conflicting events, policies and actions in the larger ecosystem.

Chapters 1, 6 and 7 are admittedly unusual in a work of non-fiction. We made assumptions and postulated about the future, a future where fiat currency is no longer commonly used and replaced by cryptocurrency. By doing so, we are encouraging you, the reader, to assess for yourself the present state and future of the financial system we currently depend on.

Chapter 1

A Crypto Future

Year 2153

It could very well be the easiest job in the galaxy. Undisturbed, he works every day in absolute silence. No interference from pesky colleagues; never does he have to deal with new, unexpected requests from his superiors. Nothing but feeling the air that passes through his nostrils every time he respires through his space work suit; he almost cannot even hear himself breathe. Even the relentless drilling and excavating that goes on ceaselessly around him, which he is also partaking in, creates not the slightest of sound. The vast emptiness of space will swallow and stifle the most insignificant of murmurs and the most deafening of explosions. Despite all its grandeur and magnificence, space does not even let Mahout hear the sound of his own heartbeat. The vibrations he feels within his chest during his rest breaks when he is not drilling is the only reminder to him these days that he is still alive *and* human.

That remarkable characteristic—being human, may no longer be used to describe Mahout in a few years' time. Even now, Mahout is not entirely human—at least not in the way it was regarded to be by the now technologically archaic 21st century. He has a pair of robotic legs. Mahout lost his human lower limbs just fifteen years ago. The cartilage and meniscus in both knees were too worn out for his knees to be of any productive use to the asteroid mining industry that he works in. And he is all the better for having amputated them and getting a partial humanoid upgrade. His new robotic legs fashioned from titanium will easily last him another century at the very least. With these new metallic limbs, Mahout can walk, run and stand all day without any feeling of fatigue. Lactic acid build-up is a biological phenomenon made obsolete by the relentless march of technology. Back on Earth's *terra firma*, the last of conventional humankind—those without any prosthetic limbs or organs, are slowly but surely dying out. They constitute less than a tenth of those on the blue planet. These remaining stubborn bio-luddites are either too poor or too ignorant to change themselves to prepare for the inevitable humanoid evolution of their species. Having just passed his sixty-fourth year of existence a few weeks ago, the asteroid miner can hope to remain relevant in his labour-intensive field of work for a few more decades. He has no choice—all around him, on Asteroid I8920123D orbiting Mars, are people like himself. Some have all their limbs replaced with prosthetic ones; others have a mechanical pump for a heart; a few of them even have drill bits in place of fists on their hands. Whatever prosthetic or artificial enhancement to be a better miner one can think of can be found on the asteroid Mahout is working on. If not, they probably can be found on some other asteroid being mined in the solar system to prepare for the biggest project humankind has ever embarked on—the building of the Dyson sphere around the sun.

Drilling for iron ore on his asteroid made Mahout think of his past. In the absolute silence of his work, Mahout cannot help but rue the missed opportunities that were presented to him and his family. As an adolescent, his grandfather was a Rohingya refugee who fled Burma as government troops pillaged and burnt the village that his family had lived in for generations. After having been granted asylum in Australia, his grandfather did spectacularly well enough in school to be offered a scholarship to study physics at the Massachusetts Institute of Technology in the United States. But he gave it up to play Aussies Rules football professionally in the country. Six months into his professional career, a devastating, illegal tackle from a 200-pound player from the opposing team broke both his thighs. He could never play or walk again. Wheelchair bound for the rest of his life, he was lucky enough that an Australian girl of Sri Lankan descent agreed to be his wife. Mahout's mother was an only child and she was conceived through in-vitro fertilisation. She was a robust and attractive woman who had no lack of admirers. When she was an undergraduate in New South Wales, she met the only son of a mining tycoon and they fell in love. A few months after they graduated (they were both of the same age), she was pregnant with Mahout. Despite the protests from the tycoon's family (they took serious issue with the obvious huge gulf in socio-economic status), Mahout's father went ahead to plan for the wedding anyway. However, tragedy struck a few weeks before the big day. His father died instantly when the motorcycle he was riding on was hit from the side by a pickup truck driven at 70 miles per hour by a delivery driver high on methamphetamine. The tycoon's family had the presence of mind to cut off all ties between their son and Mahout's mother while grieving for the untimely death of their precious son. Barred from accessing her dead lover's family, Mahout's mother had to raise Mahout all by herself with some help from her own family. Mahout is painfully aware that his present lot as an asteroid miner and not a mine owner was the culmination of a series of unfortunate events.

Asteroid miners like Mahout do not get a lot of time off work. For every two weeks that they spend tirelessly and ceaselessly drilling for metal ore and mineral deposits on asteroids, they get two consecutive days of rest. And then it is back to another two-week work cycle. Their prosthetic modifications allow them to go on for much longer than conventional humans with obsolete parts could. Even so, they are often overtired and overworked but none of them dare to protest or organise strikes. The mine owners always have the option of using fully automated robots to do their work. But a landmark ruling by the United States government fifty years ago compelled all asteroid miners to have in their employment three workers of *homo sapiens* origin for every robot miner that they use. This condition can be suspended if there are not enough workers of *homo sapiens* origin to operate a mine due to any reason. The American government was fully aware of the need to find a balance between providing jobs for human workers and alleviating the urgent labour needs of asteroid mining through the use of robots. Hence, the ruling and the condition under which it can be suspended. Because of this, Mahout and his human counterparts keep their heads down and work on their tasks mindlessly every single minute. The only respite that they have is a 15-minute break for every two hours of work.

Presently, Mahout is seated on the bedrock of the asteroid he is working on and enjoying his well-deserved break. He lifts his left arm to check how much *Koins* he has. A chip the size of a rice grain under the skin of his left forearm stores all his personal information—his identity, his employment details, his address, his bank account balance, his genetic code... Like all asteroid miners, Mahout is paid in *Koins*. It is the cryptocurrency for the underclass like him. If he was not the unacknowledged bastard grandson of a mining tycoon but a possible heir apparent to the mine owner's business empire, Mahout's bank account would have been denominated in bitcoin, the cryptocurrency of the elite. It is not illegal or forbidden for people of his status to own bitcoin. But the cost of doing so is prohibitive. Now, the conversion rate is a million *Koins* for one bitcoin. It is next to impossible for Mahout to buy a single bitcoin currently as he receives only 2,500 *Koins* a month for his hard work. If only he has a bitcoin, Mahout could look forward to raising the status of his avatar on 'Parallel Life' to the highest level three days later when he gets to go off on his two-day break. Parallel Life is the fifth permutation of 'Second Life' which by now is regarded as the precursor of all virtual life computer programs. By reaching the highest level, Mahout can create new parallel universes using his own rules. Anyone who wants to enter his newly created universes will have to get Mahout's approval as well as pay him any price that he gets to set. In short, Mahout will become a virtual god in his own universe. Poor Mahout the asteroid miner could only log on to Parallel Life three days later and send his avatar into a dance club and pretend to buy another avatar a drink at the bar counter. And then, it's back to the reality of his soul-crushing work in silence. Mahout realises painfully once again that his life is marked by lost opportunities. Just fourteen years ago, he missed out on buying and owning bitcoin. If only he had heeded the advice of the time traveller back then...

Year 2139

It came without any warning. Just as the first ray from the sun warmed New Zealand's East Cape on the North Island on Easter Sunday, computers all over the world—smartphones, tablets, laptops, desktop computers, etc., simultaneously received a bizarre message on their screens. It read:

"Own bitcoins now. Or forever be damned."

These two terse sentences sparked a flurry of activity in the cybersphere. Cybersecurity gurus, anti-virus experts, avid computer programmers, hackers (both rogue and ethical) and the like all went into overdrive to find the source of the message. In their zeal to be the first to crack this mystery, the message itself was forgotten. Days went by and no one was any wiser as to who wrote the message and where it came from. On the fifth day, an astrophysicist who also happened to be a hobbyist hacker arrived at a conclusion that got everyone stumped. The message did not come from anywhere on the planet. In fact, Dr. Clarice Risanto at Caltech proved to a flabbergasted global online audience that the message could be traced to a signal that emanated from Europa, one of Jupiter's moons. What followed was another manic global episode where everyone became amok with the idea that humankind had finally made contact with aliens. While the level-headed discussed and debated on the future of humankind with this historical and unprecedented development, some literally went insane. There were mass suicides reminiscent of doomsday cults like Jonestown and Heaven's Gate. Individuals also started taking their own lives, preferring to end their existence on their own terms instead of waiting for some interplanetary life-form to descend onto Earth to commit mindless pillage, torture and murder.

Two days after Dr. Risanto's earthshattering discovery, another message appeared on the screens of all computers:

"You need some more convincing. That's understandable.
Watch your screens after this message."

For the next 24 hours, no one could believe what they saw. The first few minutes of the video image, which was being shown on everyone's screens, was that of the planet Jupiter from every possible angle. It was apparent that the video of the distant planet was accelerated to speed things up. Otherwise, it would have taken twelve years to be able to have a camera orbit Jupiter and film it. Astonishingly and remarkably, it was obvious to anyone viewing the footage that superstructures could be seen on the giant planet from space. As if anticipating everyone's thoughts, the video next zoomed in on one of the superstructures. Inside a gigantic, transparent glass dome was a liveable city. There were buildings—skyscrapers, houses, clusters of estates… Vehicles zipped about in mid-air and there were human-like life forms walking about. There were forests with trees, gardens, crop plantations, rivers and lakes just like on Earth. It was similar to any other country on our familiar planet, except that everything looked more futuristic and advanced—at least a century more, accordingly to futurists on Earth who gave their expert analysis in the media later on. Subsequently, the video panned to feature Europa. The audience on Earth gasped as they were shown a speeding comet crashing into Europa's atmosphere as if the viewers were on the comet and had been forcibly injected into Europa itself. The comet disintegrated violently upon entry and split into several tiny pieces. All at once, depending on who was asked, some saw a landscape dotted with gigantic icebergs, a few had a glimpse of wintry volcano-like structures floating amidst an ocean of liquid tinged with hues of orange and crimson, others saw marine creatures thriving underneath a thick, top layer of ice and some swore they spotted their likeness with gills and webbed palms and feet… It was too much to take in for that few seconds. The media on Earth likened it to a "well-made documentary", "a spectacular glimpse of mankind's future", "a futurist's wet dream", among other phrases used to describe that video. In the optimism and euphoria that accompanied the video, once again the core message was lost.

There was no communication from the mysterious source for another month. It was again proven by scientists that the video signal came from Europa. No one could explain why. The prevailing theory was that it was broadcast to Earth by an alien civilisation. The fact that the first message featured bitcoin was ridiculed. "It must have been a joke or an outrageous claim to get our attention", a leading news commentator said. Conspiracy theorists figured out that in order to sound credible, whoever sent the message must refer to a topic that shows that he, she or it is in touch with the current developments on Earth. And since it is a year before the last bitcoin will be mined, that message was one of the best ways to allow the message's originator to demonstrate this. Immediately following that first message, the price of bitcoin spiked by 25 percent. However, once global attention became fixated on the coming contact with an alien civilisation, the hype died down in cryptocurrency exchanges and the price of bitcoin stabilised. All in all, before the third message was received, the overall price of bitcoin in that period only increased by 7 percent.

Like a reminder of what people on Earth have forgotten, the third contact from the same source felt like a slap in the face. It came exactly thirty-two days after the second contact. This time, everyone could see and hear on their screens a human being who looked exactly like them speaking. Dressed in a short-sleeved, black and white checked shirt and blue denim jeans, the bespectacled man with light-coloured skin spoke for about five minutes. This was what he said:

> "In the future, we would no longer be using currency notes. Yes, I used the word 'We'. I am one of you. I could be a descendant of one of us watching this broadcast right now. The American greenback, the Japanese *yen*, the Euro… all the currency notes we use to trade, buy and sell goods and services right now will be a thing of the past. Where I come from, these notes are found only in museums. The future economy runs on cryptocurrencies. I am living five hundred years in the future in Europa. In fact, I am not even a human being in your traditional understanding anymore. I won't go into that as that is not why I am speaking to you now. Just know that for me to be able to cross time and space for this interstellar communication and time travel to be possible, many technological advances will have to be made.
>
> My main message is that if you do not own bitcoin in this future that I live in, you will be an underclass. There are several types of

cryptocurrencies that are used for transactions in my world right now. Bitcoin is the only one used by the elites. The other cryptocurrencies in use are created just so that the rest of the underprivileged can buy and sell simple necessities like food. To give you an example of how bad it will be is that there is a cryptocurrency called *Koins* right now in use in my time in this galaxy. Like other cryptocurrencies, it is used by the non-elites. The conversion rate of *Koins* to bitcoin is 750,000 *Koins* to one bitcoin. To buy a new vehicle in Europa, I will need just under half a bitcoin. It is almost impossible to do so because a blue-collared worker typically earns around 2,000 *Koins* a month. You can do the math and quickly realise that this condemns the ordinary worker to a lifetime of mediocre, hand-to-mouth existence. Or they could simply rack themselves neck-high in debt if they are foolish enough to buy a new car. This change will not be very far off. It has already started. Powerful governments and the elites on your planet have been quietly amassing bitcoins soon after it surfaced. They will be the ones who will live comfortable and privileged lives. If you don't start now, you, your children and your children's children will form the first pool of interplanetary poor. If you don't want to live in poverty in this new world, do what I tell you after this. I know that almost all of you doubt my identity, that I am from the future and I live on Europa. You will be convinced after this broadcast. Goodbye and good luck."

Nothing unusual happened for the next 12 hours and the media had a field day like none that they had before simply because like previously, the only certainty about that last message was its source. Other than that, all the world's experts were confounded by how the messages were able to invade every computing device on the planet simultaneously, bypassing all security protocols and safeguards. What was even more amazing was that the language spoken matched that of the owners of every device that was used for the broadcast. It was an unimaginable feat of computing. No hacker or organisation was capable of such a complex task. While everyone was fixated on the enormity and complexity of the computing effort required, the sign that the planet should have actually been waiting for, and had almost forgotten about, came. It started with a posting on an online forum by someone from Singapore asking for help and advice. He logged on to his online banking account and found that his balance was zero. There were a few helpful replies, like telling him to call his bank or refresh his Internet browser. However, the next posting by MuraliStar, the online moniker of the thread starter, was disturbing. He wrote:

"It happened to all my other bank accounts too. I have three accounts with different banks and the balance is zero in ALL OF THEM. I called all my banks and they haven't got back to me. My wife, our families and friends have just found out that their bank accounts have no money in them, like me. This was after I told them about my experience. Some of them have bank accounts not just in Singapore but in other countries as well.

Guys, you may want to check yours too. This looks very bad."

In less than half an hour, millions replied to that message chain. All reported the same phenomenon and it had become a worldwide occurrence. From Afghanistan to Zimbabwe, everyone and anyone who had a bank account saw to their horror that they had no money left in them. Even governments were starting to report that national ledgers have been reduced to zilch. So far, all the major global banks were quiet on the shocking discovery. None issued any statement and their reticence was adding to the panic. Amid this global pandemonium, no one remembered the time traveller and his message.

Chapter 2

Bitcoin—A Rollercoaster Ride

By all accounts, Autumn Radtke had everything going for her. Young, smart and talented, she was already a chief executive officer at the age of 28. The American from Wisconsin had an impressive résumé: before becoming the chief executive officer (CEO) of Singapore-based bitcoin exchange First Meta in 2011, she worked for Apple, T-Mobile, Verizon and Virgin Charter, among many others. A picture of her smiling next to Richard Branson, the chairman of the Virgin Group, can be found on Facebook. Her involvement and experience in the world of virtual currencies via tech start-ups and online games made her stand out from the predominantly male digital universe of cryptocurrencies and online gaming, where gamers used bitcoin to trade virtual goods, like weapons for example, in the early days of the digital currency.

Then, all of a sudden, Autumn's life dramatically ended in bizarre fashion. Her lifeless body was found on the roof of a garbage collection point at a public housing apartment block in Singapore on the morning of 26 February 2014. The chief executive officer had leapt from the 16th floor of the block not even five minutes by foot from the city-state's police cantonment complex which houses major police departments. This included the country's Commercial Affairs

Department responsible for looking into white-collar crime. She was pronounced dead on the spot by paramedics. It was unimaginable for many that such a successful, capable young entrepreneur in a fast-growing industry chose to end her life so tragically. A post-mortem by the state coroner ruled out foul play and the official cause of her death was multiple injuries due to suicide.

To those who saw Autumn in the last days before her suicide, it was clear that she was deeply troubled and had started to behave abnormally. The renovation contractor hired by Autumn to fix her home office testified in court that she cried and hugged him for a full 10 minutes a day before leaping to her death. She cried so hard that the fifty-eight-year-old contractor's shirt was soaked with her tears, he told the court. Teng Cher Meng recalled that Autumn was always friendly and cheerful and she would often invite him to attend her house parties. Once, they even went looking for her missing cat. Although they never found her Persian, the experience bonded the two of them. Hence, he was taken aback when two days before she died, he witnessed Autumn shouting agitatedly on the phone while pacing around her home office. She broke down and confided in Cher Meng. Even though he could not understand English very well, he knew that she was worried about money.

"I couldn't really understand her, but I heard the words 'America' and 'money not here'", Cher Meng said in court.[1]

Autumn's death coincided with the woes faced by the infamous bitcoin exchange Mt. Gox. 650,000 bitcoins worth US$500 million went missing from the exchange in the same month that Autumn took her life. Hackers exploited a vulnerability in bitcoin's software to trick exchanges like

Mt. Gox with false transaction codes to make multiple false requests for payment. On 28 February 2014, the exchange, which was touted as the world's first major bitcoin exchange and at one point in time handled eight in ten of all bitcoin trade, filed for bankruptcy. Needless to say, investors dumped bitcoin following this debacle. $3 billion was lost as the price of bitcoin plunged by as much as 32 percent during this crisis.[2] There is a theory that Autumn's death was linked to the problems faced by Mt. Gox. According to Russia Today's exclusive source William Mook, Autumn (together with some others), had found some of Mt. Gox's missing bitcoins. However, Autumn and her associates, together with websites associated with the recovery effort, "disappeared".[3] It was as if some dark forces unknown to the public were operating behind the scene, executing those involved and shutting down websites linked to them. It was a very conspiratorial Jason Bourne-like plot which no one managed to uncover. This theory was never proven officially and could only be described as sensational and worthy of a Hollywood movie plot. Unless more credible information surfaces, we can only say that Autumn was deeply troubled by financial woes related to bitcoin which was undergoing an extremely tough time due to the problems faced by Mt. Gox around the time of her death.

Autumn Radtke's life was representative of the fortunes of bitcoin. From its inception in January 2009, one bitcoin was literally worth nothing in fiat currency. Then, in March 2010, $0.003 could buy one bitcoin. Two months later, it was valued at less than one cent. In July 2010, its value rose eight-fold to eight cents per bitcoin. A year later, it was worth $31—a whopping 387 times increase in value. A look at the historical price chart of this ground-breaking cryptocurrency from July

2010 to February 2018 will give us a more complete picture of its spectacular increase in valuation over time:

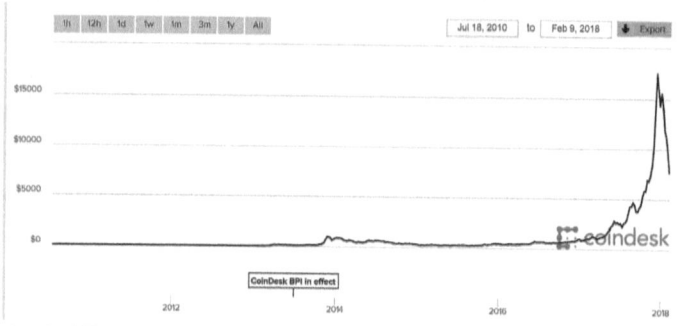

Coindesk's Bitcoin Price Index (www.coindesk.com)

If one focused solely on the short-term price fluctuations, say between 10 February 2014 and 28 February 2014 during the peak of the Mt. Gox missing coins crisis, the conclusion would be that the value of bitcoin is extremely volatile. It would be a case of "buyers beware and invest at your own risk". If one cannot ride out such crises in the short term, they may, like Autumn, choose to take drastic actions. Autumn, like bitcoin in its early years, was full of promise. Talented and capable, if only she rode out the storm and waited for the upswing, Autumn would have bounced back up, much like the V-shaped recoveries that characterised much of bitcoin's price history. Looking at the general trend, it is clear that if anyone had just 100 bitcoins right at the start when it was worth almost nothing and then held on to them over the years despite the numerous short-term price fluctuations until February 2018, one would have become a millionaire. Pretty impressive for owning something that does not really exist physically.

While this may sound like an easy way to get rich effortlessly, let's not forget the story of James Howells. Working in the information technology sector, the bloke from Newport, Wales, had the foresight to keep the hard drive of his laptop that was used to mine bitcoin. After disassembling the laptop and selling off its various parts on eBay, he kept the hard drive containing 7,500 bitcoins that he had accumulated ever since he started mining the digital currency in 2009. But strangely, in the middle of 2013, he threw out the hard drive when he was cleaning his house. At that time, a bitcoin was worth $130, which meant that the hard disk was worth $975,000. The hard drive and all the bitcoins in it were eventually dumped at a local landfill site where it has remained since. The loss: a mind-boggling $85 million based on the market valuation of a bitcoin at $11,350 in December 2017.[4] Virtually a multi-millionaire, James can only verify his claim and cash out his lost bitcoins if the Newport city council allows him to dig up the landfill. That is not an easy feat given that 350,000 tonnes of waste material are buried there. So, the next time your mother tells you to take out the trash, sift through your garbage bags carefully. You do not want to end up like James.

Stories like James involving carelessness with bitcoin are a dime a dozen. Even the editor of a technology website lost millions as he threw away a hard drive with 1,400 bitcoins in it. (Spot the pattern here?) Campbell Simpson edits the Gizmodo Australia and he bought the bitcoins for $25. About two years later, he threw away the hard drive while preparing to move homes. He lamented his loss online, stating in August 2017 that his bitcoins would have been worth $7.6 million.[5] So much for hindsight. Sometimes, it's not just about negligence. There have been cases of people being way too casual with how they spent their bitcoins. The story of how bitcoin enthusiast Laszlo Hanyecz paid 10,000 bitcoins for two pizzas worth $25 in May 2010 has become an urban legend by now. Those two pizzas must have been the most expensive ones ever in history because based on the December 2017 valuation of bitcoin, they are easily worth over $110 million. For Laszlo's sake, we sure hope that he enjoyed them down to the last bite.

The stories of Autumn, James, Campbell and Laszlo show how people all over the world are trying to handle this new-fangled technology. Not a unanimously accepted currency, not quite a commodity and definitely not even real like gold, silver and cheap metal coins, bitcoin holds a lot of promise but at the same time it comes with several pitfalls. If one is careless, like James or Campbell, one may suffer huge paper-losses and may forever rue the lost opportunities. If only… In Autumn's case, the inability to cope with business losses from the unpredictability of bitcoin might have contributed in part to her tragic decision to end her own life while she was in her prime. Today, it will be unthinkable for anyone to fork out even one bitcoin for a pizza, let alone 10,000. Unregulated and unprecedented in history, bitcoin territory is much like the American Wild West. With some luck, you may have lots to gain; otherwise, venture at your own risk. Like in the Wild West, be prepared for nasty surprises.

Chapter 3

The Digital Wild West

In the final shootout scene in the Oscar-winning Western *Unforgiven*, the fatally wounded local sheriff played by Gene Hackman bitterly said to William Munny, the 1992 film's protagonist played by Clint Eastwood, while lying helplessly on the floor: "I don't deserve this... To die like this. I was building a house." Clint Eastwood's character replied coldly: "Deserve's got nothin' to do with it," before shooting the sheriff and sending him to meet his maker. These iconic last words uttered by the sheriff exemplify the state of the cryptocurrency world dominated by bitcoin. Just like the push to the West and the subsequent gold rush seen in various parts of the United States in the 19th century, the uncharted terrain of bitcoin comes with attractive promises that are accompanied by unseen perils. The story of how some 300,000 people poured into California following the discovery of gold by James W. Marshall at Sutter's Mill in Coloma in January 1848 is known to almost every American child. When the Californian Gold Rush began, California was technically still under Mexico. It was occupied militarily by the United States due to the Mexican-American War and only formally incorporated into the Union as a new state in September 1850. Until its incorporation, California was literally a lawless place. It was finders, keepers and anything goes in the mad rush to get rich. Laws were scant and justice was often brutal and harsh, delivered from the guns of bounty hunters, sheriffs and their deputies, not unlike those we often see in Westerns like *Unforgiven*. One can work hard to make a living, try to get rich and "build a house", so to speak, like Gene Hackman's character in the movie. But in the Wild West, everything that one owns, including one's life, can be taken swiftly from anyone just because. "Deserve's got nothin' to do with it."

The world of cryptocurrency is very much like that. Like most gold rushes, the first people to mine for gold get first dips and usually anyone who arrives after the first wave are just looking for scraps or they just take a lot longer and expend more effort doing so than the pioneers. This was seen in the Californian Gold Rush as those who started mining from 1849 onwards had to put in disproportionately more time and effort than those who had mined and gotten their rewards a year earlier. The mysterious creator of bitcoin, Satoshi Nakamoto, has a million bitcoins to his name and he spent a lot less time and effort amassing them than the bitcoin miners today who have to invest in expensive hardware and even open up bitcoin "farms"—sophisticated setups with the fastest state-of-the-art computers and cooling machines to prevent overheating in an ever increasing race to accumulate bitcoin before the last bitcoin is mined (like gold, the supply of bitcoin is finite). At least miners put in effort regardless of the nature of their reward—gold or digital currency, to get what they want. There are others who have come up with other means to lay their hands on what others have worked hard for. This is the digital Wild West where laws governing cryptocurrency are almost non-existent and everyone—from politicians and bankers to the average person, are still grappling with it. And as in anything or system where rules are not in place, the potential for exploitation is huge.

The rapid, exponential surge in the price of bitcoin that was discussed in the previous chapter meant that many, even those without a clue what exactly bitcoin is, rushed into buying the cryptocurrency without understanding anything about it at all. All they could see was something that could potentially make them a lot of money in a very short time. The lure of quick returns meant that people let their guard down and abandoned common logic and rationality in the hope of getting rich quickly. Schemes, or as some say, scams, like Bitconnect, exploit this weakness. The facts surrounding Bitconnect are nothing short of startling. As of February 2018, Bitconnect collected at least $1 billion from thousands of people.[6] To put matters into context, Bitconnect was founded only about three years earlier. What is even more shocking is that no one knows who or what is behind Bitconnect. Imagine this: Lots of people giving away tonnes and tonnes of money to an unknown recipient. Why not just throw money into a bottomless pit? It is *that* insane. The only difference (and it is really just academic) is that this travesty involves cryptocurrency.

The idea behind Bitconnect is not new. Remember Bernard Madoff? Ponzi scheme? Sounds familiar? Bitconnect relies on the same underlying principle. Investors give Bitconnect a loan and they will earn interest from doing so. Lenders can earn up to 0.25 percent daily. This means that anyone who loans Bitconnect $100,000 will get $7,601.13 in interest earnings in a month—a 7.6 percent return on investment, placing it on par with many established financial instruments like bonds, shares and commodities. So, what's the big deal? In practice, Bitconnect commits an investor who pumps in $100,000 for at least 120 days. So, on the 121st day, should the investor choose to withdraw the principal sum, he or she will earn $30,250.29—a whopping 30.25 percent return, making it an investment vehicle of outstanding value. What is even more amazing is that the "investments" have to be made in the website's own cryptocurrency called BCC or Bitconnect Coin (not to be confused with bitcoin). So, in order to make an investment, you first have to deposit bitcoin into Bitconnect and then convert the bitcoin into BCCs and then loan Bitconnect using the very same BCCs that you have just been issued from the website itself (remember, these BCCs came from the bitcoin that you had just converted). Interest payments are made to you in BCC as well. Investors will have to re-convert the Bitconnect payouts into bitcoin to realise their market value.[7] This should immediately set off alarm bells. What this means is that Bitconnect is just drawing in bitcoin and giving out BCCs which has no value outside of Bitconnect. BCC is worth something only if it can be used to buy everyday stuff like food, clothes, cars, etc. Or, like bitcoin, BCC is being pegged to the US dollar, for instance, or it is being used to trade in various virtual exchanges throughout the world. BCCs are not used anywhere else except within Bitconnect. By paying Bitconnect investors in the very same cryptocurrency that they have pumped in earlier, these investors have their investment trapped within a system recognised by none outside of it. To put it simply, they have been had. And of course, since the payout is huge, the site must get more and more funds from others. Hence, it's a pyramid scheme, a Ponzi. No real goods are exchanged and the BCCs are practically worthless. Once people realised this, it unravelled rapidly and disastrously like any money game in history. At the tail end of 2017, BCC was trading regularly above $400. But by early March 2018, the price of one BCC hovered around $2.50. This sharp drop in value came as the website announced that it was closing its lending and exchange platform in January 2018.

In the unregulated online universe of cryptocurrency investment platforms and exchanges, it may not even be obvious that one's investment could be in danger. One such online platform is Yobit. At a glance, Yobit functions very much like any real or virtual exchange. Just like forex trading, Yobit allows investors to buy and sell their investment of choice (in Yobit's case, these are the various cryptocurrencies like bitcoin, litecoin, dogecoin, etc.,). It is all very convenient and enables buyers and sellers of cryptocurrencies to either cash out (only in US dollar, though) or convert from one cryptocurrency to another (from bitcoin to ethereum, for instance). Founded in Russia in 2014, Yobit offers convenience because of convertibility. However, the Moscow-based exchange suffers from a severe lack of credibility. No one knows who is behind Yobit and its customer support is as good as non-existent. Numerous complaints have been posted online about how cries for help with regard to various issues have gone unanswered. Another huge dent in the exchange's trustworthiness is that it lists any and all cryptocurrencies out there, even if a particular cryptocurrency is unreliable or an outright scam. It still allows BCC to be traded despite the numerous huge red flags and unanswered questions hanging over this dubious cryptocurrency. It's like having a well-known Ponzi scheme traded on the NASDAQ or the London Stock Exchange. Yobit does not conduct any due diligence on the cryptocurrencies that are being traded on it and so, literally, it is "traders beware". If a trader buys and sells a cryptocurrency that is nothing but a scam, Yobit will not be responsible for it and it simply does not care.[8] In fact, Yobit even allegedly traded crypto-tokens issued by the Waves platform even before the tokens could be withdrawn from private Waves digital wallets. Simply put, Yobit tried to trade a digital currency that was not even available for trading by the organisation that produced the currency. To protect its interests, Waves issued a public statement in 2016 that read: "Please note that currently Waves coins cannot be withdrawn from a personal account at the ICO (Initial Coin Offering) website; therefore, they cannot be transferred to any exchange."[9] That was all Waves could do in this possible scam by Yobit. This is because no one knows where to locate Yobit's owners or its administration. There is no legal recourse or any recourse of any kind for that matter. A positive development was that Russian authorities have started to take legal action against Yobit due to alleged fraud. As a first step, the Russian telecommunications regulator Roskomnadzor blocked access to Yobit from Russian IP addresses in early 2017.[10] But in the largely unregulated world of cryptocurrency trading and investment, there are several hidden dangers for those hoping to get rich quick like the gold miners of yore.

It is said that imitation is the highest form of flattery. With the success of Satoshi Nakamoto's bitcoin, it is hardly surprising that other cryptocurrencies like ethereum, litecoin, dogecoin and others (categorised as alt-coins) have surfaced. None of these alt-coins have used "bitcoin" as their moniker for obvious reasons. Otherwise, how would anyone know the differences between and among all these cyber coins if they too use bitcoin as part of their name? Product differentiation is key to brand identification—that is Marketing 101. Perhaps, that is precisely why a new alt-coin surfaced in August 2017 and it was called bitcoin cash. Underpinning bitcoin's success and versatility is the open-source software that allows anyone to modify the blockchain coding that guarantees bitcoin's reliability. This meant that there is no patent or copyright that prevents anyone from using the same technology behind the cryptocurrency and this lack of legal ownership extends to the name of the landmark digital currency. Hence, nobody in the world could say that bitcoin cash posed an infringement of any sort. (By the way, for any such copyright ownership or patent to be filed, someone has to make the legal claim and this would mean outing Satoshi Nakamoto's true identity. And this is not likely to happen). A comparison can be made here with manufacturers of 4x4 off-road vehicles. They simply cannot call them jeeps just because Jeep as a company has a copyright over the use of the word "jeep" in the marketplace. Similarly, a company that produces and sells in-line skates that is not legally registered as Rollerblade cannot name and market its products as rollerblades because the name of this product has already been owned legally by (yes, you guessed it) the company Rollerblade. So, in this crypto-jungle emerged a similar sounding alt-coin named bitcoin cash. No wonder bitcoin enthusiasts have been crying foul over this nomenclature which may confuse and mislead those who are not in the know. After all, since bitcoin itself can be converted or traded for cash, what then is the difference between bitcoin and bitcoin cash, especially for those who are just venturing into the cryptocurrency space just to make a quick buck or two?

To further complicate matters, bitcoin and bitcoin cash share a history that goes deeper than having similar sounding names. Bitcoin cash (known as BCH on cryptocurrency exchanges and called Bcash by some) is an offshoot of bitcoin. Bitcoin cash branched out from bitcoin's blockchain in what is known as a hardfork. Think of a taxi driver who is only allowed to drive his taxi in one direction on a highway with only one lane or carriageway. Also, he can only drive at a speed of 10 miles per hour, no more, no less, and he can only take one passenger per journey. The conditions that this taxi driver operates under are similar to the conditions that govern bitcoin's blockchain ledger. Before bitcoin cash was created, there was only one single bitcoin blockchain ledger (the highway with only one lane, travelling in one single direction) and the bitcoin network could handle only about seven transactions per second (taxi's speed of 10 miles per hour). Every 10 minutes, a node on the blockchain could also only process one megabyte of data (only one passenger per journey). To some, these limitations of the original blockchain were not ideal. They wanted the blockchain to be able to handle more data per node and process transactions faster (i.e., have the taxi driver going faster and take more passengers per journey). That is when the hardfork happened. With bitcoin cash, the taxi driver could now drive off the highway (take a fork in the road), drive faster and fetch more passengers each time. Now, sticking to the taxi driver analogy, there are now two routes and two different taxi drivers. The first one—the original taxi driver, stuck to the same route and operated under the original conditions. That is bitcoin (or some say bitcoin classic to avoid confusion with bitcoin cash). The second driver took the fork in the highway and is now driving along the second, separate route created by the fork. This second driver could now drive faster and take more passengers. This second driver is analogous to bitcoin cash. Since the hardfork, bitcoin and blockchain became separate, just like how there are now two different taxi drivers (bitcoin and bitcoin cash) and two different routes (two different blockchain ledgers). Bitcoin cash was developed because some within the cryptocurrency community wanted to change the original conditions bitcoin was operating under. The supporters of the hardfork felt that the original bitcoin blockchain processed transactions too slowly as the data it handled per node was too little.

This is where conspiracy theorists have their field day. At the time the hardfork took place, anyone holding any amount of bitcoin would receive the same amount in bitcoin cash. For example, if you owned 1,000 bitcoins (as units of the cryptocurrency and not its prevailing dollar value) at the time of the hardfork, you would also receive 1,000 units of bitcoin cash and still keep the 1,000 bitcoins you originally have. So, is this a ploy to replace bitcoin with bitcoin cash not just by having a similar sounding name but also by opting for the hardfork that will flood the cryptocurrency space with more bitcoin cash (which can process transactions faster and handle more data) than bitcoin? Some will say yes. To understand why there are conspiracy theorists deriding bitcoin cash, we have to look at two personalities in the world of cryptocurrency—Roger Ver and Jihan Wu.

First of all, it is very strange that the domain name bitcoin.com is owned by Roger Ver. Well, that's fine except that bitcoin.com deals only in bitcoin cash. As if sharing a similar sounding name isn't enough, anyone hoping to buy bitcoin may logically log on to bitcoin.com and end up buying bitcoin cash and not the original bitcoin. Being one of the pioneers of cryptocurrency, Roger Ver's fervent advocacy of bitcoin has earned him the moniker "Bitcoin Jesus". He was the chief executive officer of Memory Dealers, a firm that purportedly manufactured computer hardware, and it was one of the first firms to accept cryptocurrency as payment. He has also invested over a million dollars in startups related to bitcoin like Ripple and Blockchain.info. Additionally, "Bitcoin Jesus" donated more than $1 million worth of bitcoin to the US-based Foundation for Economic Education. Despite his philanthropic tendencies and intrepid spirit, Roger Ver is no Satoshi Nakamoto. Unable to get the majority of the bitcoin community to agree to increase the block size limit of bitcoin's blockchain, Roger Ver backed the decision to have the hardfork that created bitcoin cash. Financial commentator Max Keiser best summed up the indignation of the critics of this hardfork with this quote:

> "Bitcoin cash is an alt-coin that has its fans just like many alt-coins. I don't think anyone who uses bitcoin's name and applies it to an alt-coin like bitcoin cash does is adhering to acceptable business practices. In other words, bitcoin's brand is being stolen by a competitor that calls itself bitcoin cash and this is outright fraud in my opinion, just like it's fraudulent to use Coca-Cola and Nike's name to sell soft drinks or shoes."[11]

No one should realistically expect Roger Ver to represent orthodox business practices, given that he said that insider trading is a "non-crime" during an interview with CNBC in December 2017.

To complete the circle, the relationship between bitcoin cash and the Chinese cryptocurrency community must be explored. The key figure will be Jihan Wu, the co-founder of Bitmain. Bitmain is a cryptocurrency mining company that is headquartered in Beijing, China. The company also produces and sells the very successful Antminer mining hardware which is specifically designed for only one purpose—to mine bitcoin and alt-coins as efficiently as possible. Compared to all other mining hardware on the market, Antminers are the most efficient in terms of power usage. This is extremely vital as bitcoin mining requires a lot of electricity. By lowering the costs of electricity used, Antminers soon became the industry standard in cryptocurrency mining. It is estimated that seven out of 10 devices used to mine bitcoin are Antminers. With industry-leading equipment, Bitmain is able to assemble and bring together the most efficient mining hardware and focus all its efforts to solve the complex mathematical puzzles needed to get the reward of the various cryptocurrencies it is after. Since it makes its own mining hardware, Bitmain is able to set up its mining pools using equipment it produces and owns. In this business model, Bitmain can achieve lower costs compared to its competitors. It comes as no surprise that Bitmain is a leader in the world of cryptocurrency mining. The Beijing-based company owns the world's two largest mining pools—BTC.com (largest) and Antpool. Bitmain is also an investor in ViaBTC, the world's third-largest mining pool. Together, these three mining pools represent half of the world's mining power dedicated to bitcoin mining. Which means to say that Bitmain is very influential in the world of cryptocurrency mining. That is not all. Besides being a mining leader with industry-standard hardware, Bitmain theoretically can control all the Antminers even if they are not owned by Bitmain. In April 2017, it was revealed that a vulnerability in the Antminer software meant that Bitmain could remotely shut down any Antminer anywhere in the world just because it wanted to.[12] Named Antbleed, this backdoor meant that even if someone has bought an Antminer online using his own hard-earned cash and set it up in his home, Jihan Wu could simply just shut it down with no reason given. With more than half of the world's mining network using Antminers, this meant that Bitmain effectively controlled the global mining network with this not-so-secret power that it has. In theory, Antbleed allows Jihan Wu to keep the miners that Bitmain has influence over running seamlessly and obediently while condemning the rest of the miners outside of Bitmain's circle in cyber purgatory.

Logically speaking, fans and supporters of the original bitcoin should support the hardfork, given that it would allow the blockchain to process transactions eight times faster because of the larger block size limit (from 1MB to 8MB). Why would they not want the blockchain to be better at handling data? This improvement would enable bitcoin to realise its goal of becoming the transactional mode of choice that may one day replace paper money. It is precisely because of what some saw as Jihan Wu and Bitmain's disproportionately large role in bitcoin cash that they resisted the hardfork and bitcoin cash. With Jihan Wu's huge influence over the bitcoin cash network, Satoshi Nakamoto's vision of empowering individuals with bitcoin so that they will no longer be subjected to the vagaries of politics and government policies behind nations' monetary decisions will be lost. No one person should have enough power to control bitcoin and that is why blockchain was built upon open-source software. Such empowerment will not be achieved if bitcoin cash becomes the cryptocurrency of choice. In this scenario, Jihan Wu will become the god of cryptocurrency and Roger Ver will be right by his side as the false messiah. The potential for market and price manipulation will be impossible to ignore with such dominance; do not forget that there is no central authority governing investment behaviour with regard to cryptocurrency anywhere in the world. A case in point will be how Coinbase suspended trading in bitcoin cash as soon as the San Francisco-based cryptocurrency exchange offered the spinoff to its investors in December 2017 due to suspected insider trading. The price of a unit of bitcoin cash spiked to $8,500 on Coinbase and its affiliated exchanges while it remained at $3,500 on other exchanges. This compelled Coinbase chief executive Brian Armstrong to publicly state that all "Coinbase employees and contractors were explicitly prohibited from trading Bitcoin Cash and from disclosing our launch plans over a month ago. This was communicated multiple times via multiple channels to employees".[13] What happened at Coinbase is just a microcosm of the global cryptocurrency ecosystem. If it can happen at one exchange, why won't it occur in the worldwide trade of bitcoin cash that is dominated by only a few major players as seen earlier?

It therefore comes as no surprise that bitcoin cash has come under intense fire. Jonathan Hamel, a bitcoin and blockchain consultant, said in the Canadian Parliament in March 2018:

"It is important to distinguish between Bitcoin and the various other cryptocurrencies in circulation. Bitcoin is considered by the industry and the North American regulators to be a commodity-like asset, such as gold, and to have currency-specific properties, such as divisibility, liquidity, *transactability*, and fungibility. But let's be clear: Bitcoin it [sic] not a currency. Bitcoin is also not a security. Some other cryptocurrencies, like Ether, are more like securities, and the regulators are currently paying close attention. Other cryptocurrencies are downright scams, like Bcash… Bitcoin is a serious industry that is developing at a fast pace in Canada despite the lack of institutional support."[14]

Whether it is Bitconnect, Yobit or bitcoin cash, the signboard at the side of the road screams "Buyers beware!" Indeed, like William Munny said: "Deserve's got nothin' to do with it." Some light a fire and cook a sumptuous meal; others do the same and get burnt. For better or for worse, Satoshi Nakamoto lit a fire and it has become so huge that national governments can no longer ignore the flames. It is to this that we turn to in the following chapter.

Chapter 4

Tulip Bulbs

"You all can do whatever you want and I don't care."
"If you're stupid enough to buy it, you'll pay the price for it one day."
"Who cares about bitcoin?"
"Governments are going to crush it one day."
"This is the last time I'm ever going to answer questions about bitcoin because I really don't care."

When someone like Jamie Dimon gives the world advice about anything related to investments, we should pay close attention. After all, he is the chairman and chief executive officer of JPMorgan Chase. The leading global financial institution with a history of over 200 years boasts of assets worth $2.5 trillion, putting it on par with the United Kingdom which is the fifth-largest national economy by gross domestic product (in comparison, the market capitalisation of bitcoin is less than $100 billion). As Dimon said, why should JPMorgan care about bitcoin when the firm moves $6 trillion around the world every single day? So, we should listen to and follow his advice, yes? Common sense would dictate so. Those words of wisdom were uttered by Dimon at an Institute of International Finance conference in October 2017.

This is consistent with his position just a month earlier. Dimon reportedly told the media during another conference in September 2017 that he would fire any trader in his firm "in a second" if they were ever found to be trading bitcoin. He likened the craze over bitcoin to the tulip mania phenomena in 17th century Holland, when people traded in tulip bulbs and in some cases, a bulb could be traded ten times in a single day. Fortunes were made and lives were broken from buying and selling the innocuous tulip bulbs back then. Therefore, it came as a shock to many when it was revealed that JPMorgan helped its clients buy bitcoin. This was made known in the very same month that Dimon announced that anyone in his bank would be fired if they so much as trade a bitcoin. To be sure, JPMorgan did not buy bitcoin per se in this instance. Instead, it acted as an agent for Bitcoin XBT, which is an exchange-traded note that tracks the value of bitcoin. According to JPMorgan spokesman Brian Marchiony, such trades are "not JPMorgan orders" because these "are clients purchasing third-party products directly". If this is the case, then how is it different from the trade in tulip bulbs in 17th century Holland? No one actually bought or sold the bulbs themselves. Rather, contracts were drawn up to buy and sell the tulip bulbs. It was something like a futures market based on the prices of the bulbs. So, in JPMorgan's case, the firm helped its clients trade in a bitcoin exchange-traded note which, by the way, was still based on the price movement of bitcoin. Whether it is bitcoin or tulip bulbs, the essence of such trade is pretty much the same. It seems that JPMorgan does care about bitcoin and its derivatives, after all.

If the tulip mania had infected one of the largest private movers of money globally, what about national economies?

What is the world's largest economy doing about bitcoin? With a gross domestic product value of $18.6 trillion in 2016, what the United States government does with regard to bitcoin or any financial instrument should be way more instructive than what JPMorgan has said or done. And of course, it is common knowledge that financial markets and national governments all over the world closely study the economic policies and financial regulations of the world's largest economy. After all, the cliché that when the United States sneezes, the world catches a cold, is still very much relevant even in an age when economic power is also being shared with influential players like Germany, China and Japan. So, what has Uncle Sam done so far to deal with the cryptocurrency Wild West?

It comes as no surprise that regulation of bitcoin in the United States is necessitated by crime. Boom towns need their sheriffs to manage the riff-raff and protect the citizenry from the outlaws. Once the anonymity of bitcoin and the ease and fluidity of its use (access to the Internet is all that is needed) are known, it did not take long before criminal elements started to exploit bitcoin for their own ends. Transactions on the infamous and notorious Dark Web site Silk Road for forged documents, illicit drugs, weapons and even assassinations, were conducted using bitcoin precisely because the novel cryptocurrency offers anonymity. Transactions were completely untraceable. Bitcoin became the much sought-after mode of exchange that criminals dreamt of since crime surfaced. Although Silk Road's founder and owner Ross Ulbricht was busted (the US Federal Bureau of Investigation shut down Silk Road in October 2013), the numerous transactions of illicit items and services remained unaccounted for. Arresting the ringleader of a black market does not equate to arresting all those who took part in the uncountable deals made in the market itself. In any case, the arrest of Ulbricht meant that the bitcoins he owned were confiscated by the United States government. The sting operation that took place in a public library in San Francisco was perfectly timed such that federal marshals got to Ulbricht's unlocked and unsecured laptop, allowing them full access to his digital wallets that held 175,000 bitcoins. That was two percent of all bitcoins in circulation at that point in time. In an 18-month period, over four separate auctions, United States marshals sold Ulbricht's bitcoins and made $66 million.[15] While most commentators made a joke of how the authorities in the United States have lost out in the auction of Ulbricht's bitcoins (if they were sold in January 2018, they would have brought in $2.1 billion), the key point was that by auctioning off bitcoins (and those seized from a suspected criminal, no less) the government of the United States have in fact legitimised bitcoin. Will law enforcement agencies auction off to the public items seized from suspects that are illegal? When was the last time we had a public auction of heroin after a drug cartel was busted in a territory where those substances are illegal?

It is instructive to note that so far, in the country where bitcoin was "founded" (this concept itself is problematic and ironic since the cryptocurrency itself exists in the virtual world and is not bounded by physical territory), the United States government has been almost quiet on any laws or regulation concerning bitcoin. So far, there has been no outright ban and there are no indications that such a move is on the table. A lot is at stake—just in 2017, the value of Initial Coin Offerings (ICOs) went over $4 billion (bitcoin is not the only cryptocurrency used in ICOs), an all-time high.[16] ICOs are the latest way to raise funds—think of them like a mix of Initial Public Offerings (IPOs) and crowdfunding, just that everything is done using cryptocurrencies like bitcoin and ethereum, among many other types of cryptocurrency. Once again, when there is a lot of money to be made, scammers will move in. After all, it is still the digital Wild West. Uncharted and unregulated, it is perfect for dubious ICOs like Dallas-based AriseBank which claimed to have raised $600 million in just two months. The United States Securities and Exchange Commission (SEC) put a stop in January 2018 to this ICO offering that was started a month earlier by what was touted as the world's first decentralised bank. AriseBank claimed to have purchased an FDIC-insured bank. This meant that the United States government will protect anyone who deposits their assets with AriseBank with deposit insurance and hence raise its credibility with potential investors. However, this was a false claim. As if this red flag was not enough, the virtual bank refused to disclose the criminal background (if any) of its main executives. Calling it a scam outright, the SEC obtained a court order to protect retail investors from losing their money to AriseBank.[17] Along with AriseBank, several other ICOs have been called out by the SEC to be fraudulent. Using a mix of celebrity endorsement and big claims, dubious ICOs like Centra and Plexcoin lured $32 million and $15 million worth of investments, respectively. Champion celebrity boxer Floyd Mayweather Jr. was used to market the ICO by Centra Tech Inc. Centra claims to have its debit card backed up by Mastercard and Visa, a claim refuted by the SEC.[18] Not to be outdone, Plexcorp, the firm behind Plexcoins, promised its investors a whopping 1,354 percent profit in under a month.[19] No wonder the SEC clamped down on it as it could possibly be one of the most outrageous return on investment made by a financial institution in history.

It is heartening to see that the SEC has formed a cyber unit dedicated to tackling the issue of cryptocurrency fraud.[20] Still, there are no rules regarding cryptocurrencies. With bitcoin as the leader, what the United States does or does not do with it will be a benchmark for all other cryptocurrencies. So far, the law has been silent on bitcoin in the Land of the Free. There are some discussions underway but there is yet to be any statute or legislation enacted to formally regulate or monitor bitcoin and by extension, cryptocurrency.[21] Closing down scams and bogus ICOs are not the same as regulating bitcoin or cryptocurrencies. Such scams and dubious ICOs are merely the ways in which con artists go about their illicit business dealings and cryptocurrencies are just the mode of exchange used. Imagine if governments ban all usage of paper money just because Charles Ponzi used money to facilitate his notorious idea. Being the *de facto* leader of all cryptocurrencies, what the United States government does or plan to do with regard to bitcoin will be the benchmark for how it may treat all cryptocurrencies. As seen earlier, by auctioning off bitcoins taken from the course of criminal investigation, the United States government has endorsed and legitimised the existence of virtual currencies. Without specific laws or regulations, the future of bitcoin and other cryptocurrencies may reside in a grey area in the United States.

Paying for dining and shopping in any major city in China is a breeze. Consumers do not even have to bring their wallets or purses out with them. It is quite common to hear the Chinese say that "one can afford not to bring a wallet when leaving the house but one cannot do without a smartphone".

This is because of the almost ubiquitous WeChat application as well as the ease in which mobile electronic payments have been accepted and used in the world's second-largest economy. Think of the WeChat app like Whatsapp, and a lot more. Like in Whatsapp, users of WeChat create a profile, upload their pictures onto the app and they start filling up their contact lists with the phone numbers of their friends, relatives and colleagues. Then, they start sending each other voice and text messages, and of course photos and videos as well. That is just the beginning of the wonderful world of WeChat. The Chinese app with 963 million active users (as of the second quarter of 2017)[22] would not have been so popular if it kept to this tried and tested formula used by almost all other instant messaging apps (Whatsapp and Facebook Messenger each has about 1 billion active users). WeChat developed a feature that kickstarted and entrenched its appeal in the Chinese market. During the annual Spring Festival (also known as the Lunar New Year) in China and also observed in most Chinese communities outside of mainland China, it is customary for elders to give red packets (money placed in red envelopes) to the younger generation. Historically and traditionally, the gifting of the red packet is done face to face. With WeChat, even if one's parents are away in another city and there is no chance of meeting up during the festive period (due to work, failure to book transportation during the extremely busy period of inter-city travel, or for whatever reason), it is still possible to receive the red packets. In this case, the money will be sent as a virtual red packet through WeChat. That was the killer move made by WeChat during the 2014 Spring Festival. 16 million red packets were sent electronically that year and in the following year, the number hit 1 billion.[23] Up until that point in time, Alipay was the undisputed leader of the Chinese mobile payment space. Owned by the Alibaba Group helmed by the self-made multi-billionaire Jack Ma before his retirement in 2018, Alipay used to be responsible for seven in 10 mobile payments in China in 2015. It was no mean feat on the part of WeChat Pay by Tencent Holdings to chip away Alipay's market share in the world's largest mobile payment market worth $5.5 trillion. The magic of mobile payments in China lies not just in sending money electronically to people that one knows intimately. In a restaurant, at a clothing store or even at a nondescript mom-and-pop fruit stall by the roadside, the Chinese have been using WeChat and Alipay to settle their payments. For example, all one has to do to pay for a watermelon worth RMB 5 (about $0.80) at a fruit stall in Beijing is to wield a smartphone and a bank account linked to WeChat Pay or Alipay. To make a payment, the buyer just needs to scan the merchant's QR Code using a smartphone. Finally, the consumer will enter on the smartphone the amount that he owes the merchant and the payment is done. It's very convenient and hassle-free. In fact, the whole process can be so seamless that a diner in a restaurant can use WeChat Pay or its rival Alipay to order food and make the electronic payment after the meal. Asking for a physical menu these days in a restaurant in mainland China can make one seem somewhat like a country bumpkin who has not kept pace with the latest developments in society.

What does all this have to do with bitcoin in China? Plenty. If the Chinese already have a well-accepted and thriving method to transact payments electronically, why will they want to use bitcoin for the same purpose? After all, isn't bitcoin designed to settle payments in the first place? Since cash (the Chinese *renminbi* in this case) has already been widely accepted as the medium of transaction and also recognised and backed up by the Chinese government, why would the ordinary Chinese person ditch their hard-earned cash and go for something that not many understand or have not even heard of?

While WeChat Pay and Alipay have revolutionised payments in huge Chinese metropolises like Beijing and Shanghai, a digital revolution of another sort has been quietly taking place in other Chinese cities. In the far-flung western Chinese province of Xinjiang and in the northern province of Inner Mongolia, mining for bitcoin has started existing side by side with a more traditional type of mining—coal mining. It is a curious mix of the digital, post-industrial economy and the old, industrial economy. Cryptocurrency miners and workers often work long hours with little time for recreation, much like their coal mining counterparts. Even with the obvious technological differences between these two types of mining, the mines are always located away from the hustle and bustle of civilisation. For coal mines, the sheer amount of excavation that is needed and the pollution they cause mean that most of the population would reside far away from them. The location of cryptocurrency mines is no different, but for other reasons. The crypto-mine in San Shang Liang industrial park in the outskirts of the Inner Mongolian city of Ordos is a typical example of these new age mines. Located amidst abandoned, half-finished factory buildings, it would have continued to exist as a ghost town if not for its role in bitcoin mining.[24] This mining facility in San Shang Liang industrial park is owned by Bitmain, the Beijing-based firm that is a global manufacturer of bitcoin mining machines. Like in bitcoin mines in other parts of the world, the setup in San Shang Liang industrial park houses several computers, servers and transformers (the list goes on) in buildings that are constantly cooled to prevent these equipment that harvest bitcoin from overheating. Pooling computers together in a combined effort to get bitcoin will increase the chances of getting the cryptocurrency. Like in coal mining, more equipment and resources devoted to the digital mining effort will raise the frequency and probability of harvesting bitcoin. The amount of power needed for mining digital money is staggering. Measured in terms of processing power, China is responsible for close to 70 percent of the global effort to mine bitcoin.[25] According to another estimate, seven in 10 of major bitcoin mining pools worldwide are either based in China or Chinese-owned.[26] A 2017 study by Cambridge University found that almost six in 10 of the mining pools in the world are found in China. Regardless of the variances in the findings (which are slight in any case), the global cryptocurrency community is in unanimous agreement that China takes the lead in bitcoin mining. It is estimated that the amount of energy taken up by bitcoin mining in China is equivalent to the energy produced by three nuclear reactors, or 4 gigawatts worth of electricity.[27] It is no wonder that crypto-mines are often located far away from the main city centres to take advantage of lower rent and electrical tariffs.

It is therefore a surprising development that the Chinese authorities have started clamping down on bitcoin mining in their own backyard. Despite its global dominance and lead, the world's second-largest economy has decided to discourage mining for virtual gold. The country's top agency for regulating Internet finance, the Leading Group of Internet Financial Risks Remediation, was reported to have started to tighten the noose around cryptocurrency mines. By limiting and regulating the laws regarding land use for such mines and the price of electricity used by them, China is effectively telling cryptocurrency mine owners that they are no longer welcome to exploit the country's cheap land and electricity. Even environmental laws have been invoked to curb virtual currency mining. To prepare for this eventuality, plans have been made by mine owners to relocate to other countries where legislation and government attitudes are not as unfavourable as those in China.[28]

While China has not issued an outright ban on virtual currency mines, restricting the power supply to these power-hungry facilities is in itself a death sentence of sorts. China's strategy towards cryptocurrencies is a multi-pronged one. Without power, the mines cannot function. No mines, no virtual currencies. Yet, the very nature of this concept of digital currency controlled by no one as conjured by the elusive Satoshi Nakamoto meant that cryptocurrencies do not respect physical boundaries defined by national borders. To combat this, China has banned all ICOs. In September 2017, Beijing finally announced that all ICOs are illegal and ordered all cryptocurrency exchanges in mainland China to be shut down. This came after the Chinese government's more laid-back attitude before April 2014 when bitcoin was recognised as a "commodity" and an "asset class", although it did warn that potential investors should approach it with caution.[29] The bitcoin community and investors in China were not deterred. If bitcoin cannot be traded in China, then, like the cryptocurrency miners whose future in China looks uncertain, those who trade in bitcoin can take their business elsewhere. Indeed, that was what they did. Given the bleak future of bitcoin trading in China, investors looked across the sea to Japan. As a result of China's more draconian approach to bitcoin, Japan became the global market leader. The Land of the Rising Sun became the largest bitcoin exchange market in the world, with a market share of just over half measured in terms of trading volume, a week after China's announcement (with a trading volume of about 30 percent, the United States came in second). China's market share fell from 15 percent to under 6 percent in three days due to the nationwide ban on cryptocurrency trading.[30] What is also interesting to note is that the number of bitcoin wallets (a software that people download to store and manage the cryptocurrencies they own, much like a real physical wallet) downloaded by people in China is more than that of the rest of the world combined.[31] Putting these data together, we get the picture that most of the world's owners of cryptocurrencies reside in China. With the ban on cryptocurrency exchanges in China, these people are simply taking their cryptocurrency business to places like Japan (where bitcoin is legalised as a mode of exchange) where the regulatory climate is friendlier. China may have gotten rid of bitcoin. But it simply went elsewhere. Bitcoin does not need China to exist.

Piecing it all together, we get a strong sense that the issue in China is not about mobile payment. WeChat Pay and Alipay are completely acceptable because the transactions are conducted in *renminbi* issued and controlled by the Chinese government. Bitcoin (and the cryptocurrency class that it represents) poses an existential threat because it is not regulated and controlled by the powers that be in Beijing. Capital controls to prevent the outflow of Chinese *renminbi* is useless simply because anyone in China can buy bitcoin using methods that completely bypass governmental controls and exchange them into a foreign currency (or currencies) of their choice. And all these cryptocurrency transactions can be done anonymously. Such scenarios are bad news for the Chinese government. Think massive outflow of the national currency, currency devaluation, money laundering by criminals and corrupt government officials stashing their ill-gotten gains outside of China... The list goes on. It's no wonder that the Chinese authorities are uneasy with bitcoin.

While China appears to be exiting the bitcoin trading game, its large northern neighbour is looking for a way in. While cryptocurrency mine-owners in Inner Mongolia may be formulating their exit strategy, up north in Siberia, the Russians have plans to set up the country's largest cryptocurrency mine. In Siberia's third largest city of Krasnoyarsk, the Russians are to pump $48 million into an industrial park in the town of Divnogorsk. Locating it in Siberia makes perfect sense. Even in summer, the maximum temperature in Divnogorsk is a cool 20-odd degree Celsius. Its frigid winter will see freezing temperatures of minus 20-odd degree Celsius. This makes Divnogorsk ideal for bitcoin mines as it will keep the costs incurred to cool the mining machines to a minimum. Scheduled to be completed in May 2018, the mining facility will consume a projected 120 megawatts worth of electricity (about a third of the power generation capacity of the world's largest solar power plant in Kramer Junction, California) when it is fully operational.[32]

The project in Divnogorsk is consistent with what Russian State Duma member Boris Chernyshov said in November 2017. He announced that Russia could very well build a city in Siberia dedicated to cryptocurrency mining to provide income and jobs.[33] By taking advantage of the lower cost of electricity in the region (five times cheaper than in Moscow) and making use of hydroelectric power, the digital mining city could be Russia's ticket to enter the "race" for bitcoin. Russian President Vladimir Putin in February 2018 admitted to the importance of bitcoin and the blockchain technology behind it. He stated that he simply cannot allow Russia to be "late in the race" or else the country would be dependent on those who adopt blockchain early.[34] By stating it in such stark zero-sum terms, one cannot but be reminded of the nuclear arms race during the height of the Cold War when Soviet leader Nikita Khrushchev bluffed that the Soviet Union was producing rockets "like sausages that come out of an automatic machine". Seen from this perspective, President Putin has framed the narrative for Russia and the world—adopt bitcoin and blockchain, or else lose out. Also, by considering the issue from a national standpoint, the Russians do not see bitcoin as just affecting the economic and commercial spheres—the ramifications could be political, too.

Russia's treatment of bitcoin should therefore be seen in this regard. So far, Russia's approach to bitcoin shows more circumspection than its more populous southern neighbour in Asia simply because of cryptocurrency's huge potential not just economically, but politically as well. At first, President Putin called digital currencies an outright scam by equating them with pyramid schemes. That was in early October 2017. Possibly realising its huge potential, he retracted his position only a week later and went as far as to state that Russia could roll out its own national cryptocurrency to be named "CryptoRuble". Navigating the digital Wild West to avoid possible pitfalls is tricky and the Russians seem to be trying to find a middle ground. The Russian Ministry of Finance has plans to ban the use of bitcoin as a substitute for money in the country. This means that no one can use cryptocurrency to pay for a house or a car (for instance) in Russia. Only the *ruble* is legal tender. However, a total, outright ban would mean that Russia would lose out in the race to adopt and use bitcoin. Hence, by allowing bitcoin to be traded on official trading platforms, the country would still have its hand in the honeypot but not expose individuals to bogus schemes and frauds like Bitconnect and Yobit. By doing so, the Russian authorities can monitor and regulate the bitcoin transactions that are conducted through official channels. Instead of a free-for-all or a blanket ban, the Russian bitcoin experiment may very well allow the country to find a balance. After all, President Putin himself acknowledged after a February 2018 meeting with Herman Gref, the president of Russia's largest bank Sberbank, that Russia needs professionals in the field of cryptocurrency and blockchain because as Gref puts it, "this technology has a huge impact". A deadline of 1 July 2018 was set by the Russian President to put cryptocurrency regulations in place so that the country will put in place "very careful regulations" that would not prohibit cryptocurrency.[35] The world will have greater clarity with regard to Russia's official stance on bitcoin when that happens.

From JPMorgan to the world's largest economies of the United States and China and then looking at Russia, the country with the world's largest land mass, despite their differing and sometimes shifting stance towards bitcoin, a common pattern is emerging. The movers and shakers of the global economy do not have what it takes to subdue the bitcoin phenomenon. One can ignore bitcoin and dismiss it totally at first. But like JPMorgan's chairman and CEO

Dimon has shown, cryptocurrency is just too lucrative to be ignored and he had to eat his own words as soon as he uttered that he would fire anyone in his company if they dabbled in bitcoin. In the United States, just like anywhere else in the world, criminals would resort to anything to make a quick buck. Cryptocurrency is no different. But is it the fault of the instrument that was used to facilitate criminal activities and illegal transactions? Why not outlaw currency just because the mafia is conducting illicit businesses using cash? Similarly, bitcoin is merely the means (and it is just one such) through which crooks profit from their crime. Al Capone could very well transact using potatoes and no one in their right mind would blame potatoes for his shenanigans. So, why blame bitcoin? And by the way, just by auctioning off bitcoin seized from criminals, the United States had in fact legitimised it. In China, we could see the contradiction between reality and what the authorities want. Driving bitcoin out of China by targeting the mines and banning ICOs only meant that the world's second-largest economy would lose out in the long run. Bitcoin investors would simply satiate their craze for cryptocurrency elsewhere. This is where countries like Russia might pick up the slack left by China. By walking the tightrope between prudent regulation and total prohibition, President Putin could be ensuring that Russia does not yet again lag behind the West (as it often has throughout its tumultuous history) in technological advances. So much for a phenomenon scorned as mere tulip bulbs. And like the tulip bulb phenomenon back in 17th-century Holland, lives are made and lost in this high-stakes game. The fact that the major economies and governments of the world are thinking seriously about bitcoin is a strong indication that no one should think that the ramifications of cryptocurrency are confined within the digital space of the virtual world. A Pandora's Box has been opened by the mind of Satoshi Nakamoto. The future will never be the same once bitcoin achieves its full potential.

Chapter 5

When It Hits the Fan

It is not without irony that bitcoin and the crucial blockchain technology behind it emerged at about the same time as the subprime mortgage crisis unfurled across the United States and then the world like a hurricane from 2007 to 2009. The subprime fallout that resulted in the global financial crisis saw American financial institutions like Freddie Mac and Fannie Mae go bust. Similarly, detractors of the cryptocurrency are pointing out how the speculation in bitcoin is in itself creating a bubble. And we all know what happens when the balloon pops. The party is over and everyone realises how silly they were.

Satoshi Nakamoto (or whoever invented bitcoin) meant for cryptocurrency to be the answer to the problems that plagued the world's economy and financial markets. If reputable financial institutions can sell dubious products to unsuspecting retail investors who are no wiser, what does it say about the state of the world economy?

It is estimated by the United States Government Accountability Office that at least a staggering $22 trillion was wiped out by the subprime mortgage crisis in the United States alone. That's enough to decimate the economy of Germany, the world's fourth-largest economy, almost six times over. Now that the party is long over and everyone is sober, it is easy to say how completely insane it was to buy financial products that no one really understood and which, by the way, were rotten to the core. Simply put, would anyone in their right mind invest in a home loan given to an alcoholic who cannot even command a regular monthly income to make the payments? Yet, plenty did. Why? Simply because they placed their trust in credit ratings given by agencies which were ultimately revealed to be flawed. With interest rates hovering at the 1 percent mark after the 2000 dot.com bust, Wall Street had to get creative to earn more than the meagre returns yielded by United States Treasury bonds. High returns mortgage-backed securities became sexy financial products and the credit rating agencies—Moody's, S&P and Fitch, all gave these securities the thumbs up by giving them their highest triple-A rating. As a result, they were seen to be as safe as United States Treasury bonds. And since they offered better interest rates, the average Jane and Joe bought them like hot cakes through fund managers who did not know any better. In the unregulated private securities and derivatives market, the party went on and the bubble grew to three times the size of the global economy based on the value of the derivatives market in 2007.[36] It was only after the painful fact that everyone realised that the securities were as good as trash in the garbage. One such mortgage bond that turned sour is MortgageIT 2006-1. The asset-backed security was first offered by lender MortgageIT in 2006 and Moody's gave the bond its highest rating. After the crash, Moody's gave the same mortgage bond its fourth-lowest rating of Caa3. MortgageIT was accused by the United States government in 2011 of "reckless lending practices" in a lawsuit filed against Deutsche Bank as the bank acquired MortgageIT. Deutsche Bank paid $202 million to settle the lawsuit.[37]

The story of Citigroup during the subprime crash will be instructive of the damage done in the private commercial space. As America's largest bank and one of the largest financial institutions in the world with 3,000 branch offices worldwide in more than 100 countries, Citigroup, as a global financial behemoth, could boast that it was once the world's largest financial institution based on market value. In late 2006, just before the subprime bust, the company's share price peaked at $57 per share. But it all came crashing down in the first quarter of 2009. In March 2009, a unit of Citigroup's stock was worth less than $1. By trading as low as 97 cents, Citigroup's market valued plunged precipitously from $277 billion in late 2006 to less than $6 billion in March 2009. In a 15-month period that ended in December 2008, Citigroup chalked up $37.5 billion in losses. As a result of the crash, Citigroup's standing fell to 27 out of 81 financial firms ranked according to market value by S&P. The United States government had to step in to rescue the financial giant with rescue packages worth $45 billion in all. Exposure to bad loans at a time when investor and market confidence were jittery accounted for the financial turmoil experienced by Citigroup.[38]

By now, with the benefit of hindsight, the story of the subprime mortgage crisis resembled a house of cards. Built on shaky foundations, bad loans and bad investment decisions led to the global financial crisis. All because investors and the average person looking to increase the yields on their portfolio depended on seemingly reliable assessments by credit rating agencies. If ratings of such private securities can be shown to be nothing more than a chimera, what about the credit ratings given to sovereign nations?

The world economy since the end of the Second World War had a dependable pillar: the United States. Without the stimulus given to the rest of the world (minus the Soviet Union and its affiliates during the Cold War) in the form of foreign direct investments from the United States, stimulus like the Marshall Plan (or also known as the European Recovery Program) and the reliance on the greenback during the era of the gold standard globally, countries all over the world may not have recovered so quickly following the devastation of the last world war. Of course, let's not forget the impetus and growth enjoyed by the economies of nations worldwide with the concept of free trade and free movement of goods and services that were also championed by the United States. In addition, the global economic role of multi-national corporations headquartered in the United States, bringing technological know-how, commercial expertise as well as providing jobs leading to overall economic growth, should not be forgotten even as we sometimes lament the downside of globalisation. Therefore, it came as a shock that the credit rating given to the United States government was downgraded for the first time in history. S&P lowered its rating for the United States on 5 August 2011 to AA+ from the highest rating of AAA. This was an unprecedented development ever since S&P started in 1860. Never before has the United States government's ability to pay its debt been in doubt. This meant that the United States economy has vulnerabilities that are not expected of an economic superpower and global leader. These doubts were further confirmed by the debt ceiling crises of 2011 and 2013. Simply put, these crises cast doubts on whether Uncle Sam would be able to borrow money to finance the country's budget. Political infighting on Capitol Hill led to the impasse on both occasions. Even though the debt ceiling was eventually raised in both years, confidence in Uncle Sam was shaken. If the largest lender in the history of the modern world could theoretically not be able to borrow money to pay for its own national spending, who could smaller and less well-off nations turn to for help?

Looking at the big picture, the answer is: no one. The world economy is in debt. In fact, the size of the debt is enormous. According to the International Monetary Fund (IMF), the world owes itself $164 trillion and there appears to be no way that this debt can be serviced.[39] A look at the world's top 10 economies by gross domestic product (GDP) based on 2017 figures by the IMF will be instructive.

Top economies by GDP (Largest to smallest)	GDP (in trillions)	Gross government debt as percentage of GDP
United States	19.39	107.8
China	12.01	47.8
Japan	4.87	236.4
Germany	3.68	64.1
United Kingdom	2.62	87.03
India	2.61	70.2
France	2.58	97
Brazil	2.05	84
Italy	1.94	131.5
Canada	1.65	89.7

It is clear that most of the world's top economies (seven in 10) owe more than 80 percent of their GDP. If we take 70 percent as the threshold, the number rises to eight in 10. This means that even the world's largest economies have huge sovereign debt. In addition, the ability to service their national debts is shaky. Take the United States, the world's largest economy, for instance. We have already seen how the United States got itself into trouble twice when it was almost unable to raise its debt ceiling. When the United States government is unable to borrow more money, it simply means that it could not function as it is already borrowing more than the value of goods and services that the country is generating. Another important consequence is that it would also be unable to service its pre-existing public debt. The money owed just snowballs. China is the only country in the top 10 list that has a national debt that is less than half of its GDP. But the IMF projects that this figure will rise. Its projection for the world's second-largest economy is that its gross national debt to GDP ratio will increase to 51.2 percent in 2018. China's rising debt is but a small part of the overall problem. An examination of the economic relationship between the United States and China will point to the bigger, underlying challenges. The United States' trade deficit with China has been rising. After 1985, when the American trade deficit with the Chinese was zero, the United States has been running into trade deficits with China every single year to the extent that its trade imbalance with China is the largest among all United States trade deficits with any country.[40] Simply put, American consumers are buying more (in terms of dollar value) from China than the Chinese are buying from the Americans. China is clearly benefitting from this trade. In addition, China's holdings of United States government bonds have been rising to the point where it has become the country that has the largest holdings of American bonds. So, instead of using the greenbacks earned from trading with the United States, China is hoarding its earnings by not spending on American goods and services but saving them in the form of United States government bonds. This makes China a net lender to the United States. Putting one and one together, the United States is borrowing money from China to fund its national debt. But as seen earlier, the size of the American debt is so large that even with China's "loans" in the form of bond purchases, Uncle Sam will still owe a lot of money. Also, do not forget that we have seen how China's public debt is projected to grow. The Chinese government itself needs to find the cash to buy Uncle Sam's bonds. How will Beijing get the funds to do so? In part, from selling even more to the Americans. By now, this should look like a bottomless pit—the size of everyone's debt is just going to get bigger and bigger. This is the bird's eye view: the world as a whole owes a lot of money and even the biggest national economies have trouble paying off their own sovereign debt. So, who is going to settle the debt? Somebody has to. But who? It seems like the answer, for now, is no one.

Let's simplify the picture for greater clarity: If John produces set of currency notes and gives them to you (say, the numerical amount of all of John's currency given to you is 1,000) and everyone knows that John is in the red by 10 million, would you have confidence that John's currency would be accepted by others in the market? Would a merchant willingly and gladly accept your payment for his goods and services with John's currency notes, knowing that there is no way that John can honour them? This is the big picture for the world economy: It is $164 trillion in the red and credit ratings given to bonds and funds could be based on nothing more than a mirage and yet we do not think twice about using that currency note in our wallets—be it the American dollar, Japanese *yen*, Russian *ruble* or the Euro, to pay for goods and services. Like how no one would use John's currency notes, no one in their right mind would use any of the currency notes printed by the nations and central banks all around the world either. With the American greenback still being regarded as the *de facto* international currency of exchange even after the end of the gold standard in 1971, we still blindly believe that the largest economy in the world (which by the way owes more than it could earn) can still be the pillar of the global financial system.

If this is the case, why has the world economy not come to a grinding halt and descended into utter chaos? Well, it almost did during the subprime mortgage crisis. Without the intervention from the American government (the $45 billion aid given to Citigroup is an example), confidence in the banking system would have been further undermined. And so, the global financial system recovered, albeit slowly and never convincingly, from that episode. But this does not mean that the underlying problem has been resolved. The global debt is still there and it is growing. This is where bitcoin comes into the picture.

It was no coincidence that bitcoin came into existence around the time of the implosion of the subprime market that led to the global financial crisis. Instead of having to rely on a third party to issue the currency notes that are used to pay for goods and services (e.g. governments, central banks as third parties), why not have a system that allows individuals to pay each other using an independent method of verification? Thus, the blockchain by Satoshi Nakamoto. The enigmatic figure wrote in an email message to cryptographic experts and hobbyists on 31 October 2008: "I've been working on a new electronic cash system that's fully peer-to-peer, with no trusted third party." The blockchain itself is the method of verification. Imagine borrowing money from someone. Let's say Susan borrows $100 from Jessica. In our current financial system, it does not matter if Jessica is herself in debt. She could be in the red and still Susan can get the $100 loan from her. The current system does not care if Jessica had herself borrowed the $100 from someone else. As long as Susan gets the $100, she is happy. At the micro level, personal loans function as described. Credit cards also operate on this basis. Even with checks on one's credit history, there is no stopping Jason from applying for another credit card to pay for his existing credit card bills. And the debt owed will roll over many times. At the macro level, we have seen how national economies borrow and spend without ever having to account for the debt owed by the entire global financial system. Satoshi Nakamoto's invention aims to revolutionise payments. Before Jessica can lend Susan $100, the blockchain must verify that Jessica indeed has $100 currently at hand and that the $100 truly belongs to Jessica. In other words, Jessica cannot pretend to have the $100 or borrow the money from someone else just to lend it to Susan. Also, the blockchain must be satisfied that the $100 is not fake (like how criminals print fake currency notes to make purchases). Think of the blockchain like a series of dominoes lined up. For a transaction to be legitimate, all the dominoes must fall before the transaction can be approved. As long as even a single domino remains upright, the payment will fail.

That is the beauty and power of the blockchain technology that underpins Satoshi Nakamoto's bitcoin revolution.

How is it different from our current financial system? Satoshi Nakamoto's plan was to limit the total number of bitcoins to 21 million. In this finite system, it trumps the currency notes issued by third parties. There are plenty of examples in history to show the fallibility of transaction systems that rely on potentially infinite units. Take Germany during the interwar years for instance. To cope with the war reparations due to the Treaty of Versailles, the Weimar Republic had to issue a new currency called the *rentenmark* in November 1923. By July 1924, 500 million *rentenmarks* were in circulation. This rose to 1.8 billion in July 1924. The *rentenmark* was supposed to replace its predecessor the *mark*, which became so worthless that Germans had started to use the notes as wallpaper. By July 1924, 1.2 sextillion *marks* were in circulation. That is 1 billion multiplied by a trillion times. It led to an unthinkable situation where Germans were buying bread using *marks* carted to the shops with wheelbarrows. If one thinks the German experience to be an aberration, why not look at Zimbabwe. When the Zimbabwean dollar was first circulated as legal tender in the country in 1980, its value was on par with the American dollar. But rampant hyperinflation at a whopping 79.6 billion percent reduced the currency note to worthlessness and it was finally abandoned when the Zimbabwean government demonetised it in April 2009. At its lowest point, the Zimbabwean government printed currency notes in denominations of 100 trillion. Still, Zimbabweans could not even pay for a bus ride with a 100 trillion currency note.[41] To date, the Zimbabwean example ranks as the worst example of hyperinflation and overprinting of currency notes that wiped out any value that a currency is supposed to represent.

It is apt that Zimbabweans in recent times have finally gotten around to thinking that relying on third parties issuing currency notes for legal tender is a really bad idea. As if coping with hyperinflation was not bad enough, Zimbabweans had to put up with more privations after a military coup in late November 2017 further plunged the country's already dire economy into a deeper crisis. With more than nine in 10 unemployed, the country's economy has halved in size since 2000. Without a national currency, since the Zimbabwean dollar was abandoned, Zimbabweans have been using foreign currencies like the American dollar and the South African *rand* for their transactions. With the long-standing economic malaise and an unfolding political crisis in the country, Zimbabweans have all but lost faith in their country's ability to look after them. Unable to use banks to pay for international transactions to get much-needed goods and services in the absence of a properly functioning government, Zimbabweans decided on their own that bitcoin is a safer bet. This trend is reflected in the country's cryptocurrency exchange Golix which saw the prices of bitcoin in Zimbabwe rising to twice the amount seen in global exchanges. Bitcoin price in the African country hit $13,499 in November 2017. In a span of 30 days leading up to the military coup in November 2017, Golix processed more than $1 million worth of bitcoin transactions. This was 10 times more compared to the whole of 2016.[42] The price of bitcoin may be volatile. But compared to what Zimbabweans have experienced, the volatility of the cryptocurrency's price is still much more stable. Who said that bitcoin is nothing more than a scam? It has proven itself to be useful and absolutely vital to the people living amidst tumultuous times in the southern African nation.

Zimbabweans are not alone in turning to bitcoin during trying times. Thousands of miles across the Atlantic ocean, Venezuelans have similarly turned to digital money under difficult circumstances. Compared to 2013, the Venezuelan economy in 2017 has shrunk by just over a third in terms of GDP. On average, its people are earning 40 percent less. This puts the South American nation in a condition that's worse off than the United States during the Great Depression.[43] Inflation was almost 1,600 percent in 2017 and is projected by the IMF to hit 13,000 percent in 2018. This effectively means that the *bolivar* is nothing more than a worthless piece of paper. Ordinary Venezuelans have turned to bitcoin like the Zimbabweans. It is not nearly as bad as halfway across the world, but there is no need to hit the astronomical hyperinflation figures in Zimbabwe for the people in Venezuela to experience the harsh reality brought about by failed governments—empty shelves at stores, people rummaging through garbage bins for food scraps, resorting to desperate measures to lay their hands on foreign currencies... It got so bad that burgers could not be bought at fast food restaurants because the price of bread had become too exorbitant. It is ironic that Venezuelans have turned to something intangible even as they grasp at anything that could sustain their lives for a little longer. By turning to bitcoin trading and bitcoin mining, Venezuelans have found a way out. Using bitcoin, the desperate South Americans are able to buy daily necessities online. Since bitcoin operates on a peer-to-peer platform, Luis the shopkeeper can sell groceries and sundries to Daniela the housewife using bitcoin. And that is life in Venezuela. Thanks to cheap, subsidised electricity provided by the Venezuelan government, bitcoin mining is a hit in the country as it is the cheapest place to mine bitcoin anywhere in the world. The confluence of a bad economy and cheap electricity has made Venezuela one of the top bitcoin trading nations globally.[44]

By throwing money at the problem (i.e., printing more and more money), the Zimbabwean and Venezuelan economies simply went under. These two countries represent what the world economy in its totality is like today. How is the $164 trillion global debt going to be settled when even the world's top economies are steeped in debt themselves? In the current financial system based on the theoretically infinite supply of printed currency notes, backed up by potentially flawed credit ratings of private equities as well as governments' financial ability, the world is literally surviving on borrowed time. It is like a ticking time bomb that everyone knows is there but no one wants to deal with. Everyone except for Satoshi Nakamoto and the libertarians who, by introducing bitcoin to the world, attempt to empower individuals by circumventing the fiat currency note regime that is all too reliant on people's trust in the governments and institutions that issue those notes. Why should anyone continue to do so is the big question, after witnessing the multiple bad episodes in history that caused so much misery and hardship.

Chapter 6

Year 2140

Nobody really knows who she is. Online, she goes by the avatar Iroquois Precious. Global efforts to track her down have all but run into dead ends. The only certainty is that Iroquois Precious is the mastermind behind CryptoUnderground, the most comprehensive and reliable global cryptocurrency exchange. Even the most feared cyberhackers are not able to tell if Iroquois Precious is a real person or just a computer software that became sentient. Despite being in an era when robotics and artificial intelligence (A.I.) have hit remarkable milestones, humanity still cannot accept that Iroquois Precious might just have once been a series of codes in a computer program that decided to create an identity for itself and build a cryptocurrency exchange from scratch. But why not? By now, it is commonplace to have robots that look exactly like your neighbour with the ability to perform everyday tasks with absolute ease like washing the dishes, ironing clothes, feeding babies and cooking. Realistic facial expressions and voice intonation by robots have already become an expectation, the norm. Iroquois Precious does not operate alone—she has under her control an army of CryptoKnights who process purchase and sell orders from anyone anywhere in the world in the thriving trade of cryptocurrency. Once seen as speculative and high-risk just over a hundred and twenty years ago, trading in cryptocurrency has now become accepted as a way of life. Whether it is bitcoin, ethereum or dogecoins, almost everyone owns at least a type of cryptocurrency. It is not a question of "If you own?" but "Which one?" and "How much?"

CryptoUnderground stands out from the other exchanges because it offers not only the standard and expected anonymity of trade in cryptocurrencies; it is also absolutely reliable. In the past, dodgy exchanges like Yobit have created suspicions and frustrations because it was unable to offer reliability with anonymity. Online cryptocurrency forums have nothing but praise for how CryptoUnderground runs its business. All feedback, complaints and requests for redress have always been dealt with. It does not deal with or trade cryptocurrencies that are dubious. It was implausible that any online cryptocurrency exchange could achieve what was before thought to be an impossible balance. The speed and thoroughness in which Iroquois Precious and her CryptoKnights deal with each and every customer of their exchange arouse awe, envy and the concomitant scepticism that comes with perfection. Conspiracy theories abound that CryptoUnderground in fact records and tracks every transaction, keeping a private ledger of everyone's cryptocurrency holdings. How this information may be used has yet to be established. Narratives of such nature by conspiracy theorists only create a sense of uneasiness that someone or something is keeping score. So far, a coherent account of how this information may be misused (if it is true) has yet to surface.

On offer in CryptoUnderground are not just the classic, traditional cryptocurrencies like bitcoin, litecoin, ethereum but also a host of national coins. Just over a hundred years ago, national governments started to roll out national cryptocurrencies. Japan has it, so do the United States, Canada, Britain, Germany and Finland. In fact, most of the developed economies have their national cryptocurrency by now. Even Malaysia, Saudi Arabia, the United Arab Emirates, South Africa, Argentina, Sri Lanka and Iran have their own. China—known for its see-saw attitude towards cryptocurrencies in the early 21st century, had succumbed and jumped onto the bandwagon. The unique selling point of CryptoUnderground is that it is the only cryptocurrency exchange where anyone can request for and actually buy any and all national coins. Efforts by all national economies to prevent overtrading of their national cryptocurrencies on online exchanges have ended in failure because of Iroquois Precious and her CryptoKnights. CryptoUnderground is the only online exchange that consistently and repeatedly resisted all attempts (by national governments and other sources) to shut it down or be hacked into.

Compared to its early years, the cryptocurrency ecosystem has taken off and stabilised. People all over the world are trading goods and services using all types of cryptocurrencies. Bitcoin and the other variants that came after have replaced cold hard cash as the accepted mode of transaction. A typical visit to the supermarket does not even have to involve waiting in line to pay at the cashier. All one needs to do is make contact using one's palm with the code tag of the item they want to buy. Embedded in the centre of everyone's palm (only one) is a microchip the size of a melon seed that allows the payment to be made electronically in the cryptocurrency of their choice. In almost every major global financial centre is an automated cryptocurrency conversion hub run by artificial intelligence. These conversion hubs perform the crucial role of converting all cryptocurrencies into a common denominator that allows all electronic transactions to take place. If not, a tub of ice cream valued in Kash (a class of cryptocurrency introduced in 2088) cannot be paid by someone who owns only litecoins. And if one is so primitive to still be using the American dollar or the Japanese *yen* for instance, fortunately for them, the A.I. running the hubs can still process these transactions using the last valuation of all existing currencies (paper money) finalised in 2111. That was the year when the New United Nations (the original one having been made defunct in 2075) mandated that the world will stop using cash as the main mode of payment and transaction. A shopper using paper money will have to activate the assistance of a humanoid supermarket shop manager to access the A.I. to convert the value of their cash into cryptocurrency. It's not impossible to pay by cash in 2140; it's just a lot more troublesome.

Fundamentally, the entire cryptocurrency edifice is supported by the axiom that bitcoin is incorruptible. This original and groundbreaking cryptocurrency (with its revolutionary blockchain technology and its coding) has become regarded as the gold standard of all cryptocurrencies. The common denominator used by all cryptocurrency conversions is the value of bitcoin. The ease in which all electronic exchanges, transfers and conversions take place is achieved by basing the value of the transactions on bitcoin. This has become a double-edged sword, though. While promoting convenience, the cryptocurrency ecosystem cannot do without bitcoin which in its totality is owned by only 0.5 percent of the population. Which means to say that should this privileged bitcoin-owning elite class decide to pull the plug one day, to stop allowing the rest of the non-bitcoin owning world to convert their inferior cryptocurrencies through bitcoin, the global economy may very well come to a halt. Why they would do that is beyond anyone's imagination. Everyone's economic and commercial interests are further advanced by relying on this seamless system. If someone wants to rock the boat, they better have a more brilliant idea.

Yet, the unthinkable did happen. Just before the stroke of midnight on 28 February 2140, an anonymous post appeared on cryptowatch.org. It wrote:

> "My stash of Kash, dogecoin and litecoin are all gone. Evaporated into thin air. I stored them in my digital vault and somehow, they have vanished. Help?"

When the clock began ticking from the first second of the first minute of the first hour of the last day of February 2140, a matter of momentous, historic significance took place. In that leap year, the last bitcoin was mined. This marked the realisation of Satoshi Nakamoto's plan of having 21 million bitcoins in circulation. The process that started 131 years ago has ended; a new cycle, one that none have previously imagined, is only just being set in motion. And that cry for help on cryptowatch.org at 11:59 PM on 28 February 2140 was a sign of things to come.

Chapter 7

A Prelude

The most prevalent and accepted version of the events of the year 2139 was that it was a huge ploy to scare people into buying bitcoin to hike up its price. It was dismissed as the most elaborate attempt in history to rig financial markets. People who fervently believed in the message allegedly from Europa were treated like followers of a doomsday cult. Everyone knew about the frenzied amassing of bitcoin by groups like the Crypto Collective, the Bitcoin Commune and the Last Bit, among others. Yet, the general population never took them seriously and watched these groups with a mix of amusement and mockery. Since there was no further communication from the mysterious Europa source after that, the events that took place back then became relegated (some say deified) to the domain of popular culture, urban legend and conspiracy theory. It was the job of those apocalyptic groups to figure it out while the rest of humanity went back to their mundane and drab existence. Why should anyone accumulate only bitcoin when there are so many other types of cryptocurrencies in use?

Yet, on the last day of February 2140, the world descended into panic again. All holdings of cryptocurrencies that were not bitcoin had been wiped out. In 48 hours since the first warning sign appeared on cryptowatch.org, everyone discovered to their dismay and shock that the time traveller's message could very well be true; a few smug, anonymous individuals posted online that their huge stash of bitcoins were safe. To prove their claims, they even transferred a few *satoshis* to sceptics and posted online the screenshots of the transfers. The picture was clear to everyone: Only 0.5 percent of the population could buy anything. They could now control the world if they wanted to.

In this hopelessness, the other 99.5 percent did not know what to do. Yet, on the 75th hour since the earth-shattering realisation, Iroquois Precious posted on CryptoUnderground:

> "Trading is still ongoing here. Re-register your accounts and *all* your previous balances will be restored as if the events of 29th February never happened. This applies even to your cryptocurrency (all types) balances outside of CryptoUnderground. Do it, now."

With nothing to lose, the 99.5 percent grabbed the lifeline offered by Iroquois Precious. Whether human or A.I., she will soon be hailed as the cyber messiah once everyone's cryptocurrency balances are restored.

"The dragon stood in front of the woman who was about to give birth, so that it might devour her child the moment he was born."

Revelation 12.4

Notes

2. Bitcoin—A Rollercoaster Ride

1 Foo Jie Ying (18 September 2014), "American CEO breaks down in front of contractor day before leaping to death," retrieved 23 January 2018 from www.asia.com.

2 Paul Vigna and Michael J. Casey, *Cryptocurrency: How Bitcoin and Digital Money are Challenging the Global Economic Order* (London: The Bodley Head, 2015).

3 C. Edward Kelso (5 January 2018), "Mt. Gox bitcoin missing in relation to mysterious death of exchange CEO," retrieved 23 January 2018 from https://news.bitcoin.com.

4 Aatif Sulleyman (4 December 2017), "Man who 'threw away' bitcoin haul now worth over $80m wants to dig up landfill site," retrieved 23 January 2018 from www.independent.co.uk.

5 Campbell Simpson (28 May 2017), "I threw away $7.6 million in bitcoin," retrieved 7 February 2018 from www.gizmodo.com.au.

3. The Digital Wild West

6 Stan Higgins (20 February 2018), "US securities regulator rejects bitconnect records request," retrieved 5 March 2018 from www.coindesk.com.

7   Fitz Tepper, "Bitconnect, which has been accused of running a Ponzi scheme, shuts down," retrieved 6 March 2018 from https://techcrunch.com.

8   "Yobit Exchange: Russian Crypto Trading Platform, ICO Investing & Games?" retrieved 30 June 2018 from https://bitcoinexchangeguide.com.

9   "Be careful! Possible scam," retrieved 30 June 2018 from https://blog.wavesplatform.com.

10 William Suberg (6 March 2017), "Cryptocurrency exchange Yobit investigated in Russia on fraud claims," retrieved 30 June 2018 from https://cointelegraph.com.

11 "'Bitcoin is a gift from God to help humanity sort out mess it has made with its money'–Max Keiser" (18 November 2017), retrieved 5 July 2018 from www.rt.com.

12 James Risberg (15 April 2018), "What and who is bitmain?" retrieved 8 July 2018 from https://coincentral.com and Bennet Garner (17 May 2018), "Jihan Wu: A story of bitmain, Twitter profanity, & BCH evangelism retrieved 8 July 2018 from https://coincentral.com.

13 Simon Golstein (20 December 2017), "Pump and dump? Coinbase suspends bitcoin cash, investigates insider trading," retrieved 24 July 2018 from www.financemagnates.com.

14 Jonathan Hamel (19 March 2018), "Mr. Jonathan Hamel (President, Académie Bitcoin) at the Finance Committee," retrieved 24 July 2018 from https://openparliament.ca.

4. Tulip Bulbs

15 Jeff John Roberts (21 February 2018), "Inside Uncle Sam's secret bitcoin hoard," retrieved 22 April 2018 from http://fortune.com.

16 Steven Russolillo (14 December 2017), "Initial Coin Offerings surge past $4 billion–and regulators are worried," retrieved 23 April 2018 from www.wsj.com.

17 Roger Aitken (30 January 2018), "U.S. SEC halts alleged crypto ICO scam from 'decentralized' bank seeking $1 billion," retrieved 25 April 2018 from www.forbes.com.

18 Arjun Kharpal (3 April 2018), "Founders of a cryptocurrency backed by Floyd Mayweather charged with fraud by SEC," retrieved 25 April 2018 from ww.cnbc.com.

19 Adi Robertson (5 December 2017), "SEC charges alleged cryptocurrency scam with fraudulently raising $15 million," retrieved 25 April 2018 from www.theverge.com and Laura Shin (4 December 2017), "$15 Million ICO halted by SEC For being alleged scam," retrieved 25 April 2018 from www. forbes.com.

20 "SEC announces enforcement initiatives to combat cyber-based threats and protect retail investors" (25 September 2017), retrieved 25 April 2018 from www.sec.gov.

21 Evelyn Cheng (6 February 2018), "The US government is trying to get coordinated in its efforts to regulate bitcoin," retrieved 30 April 2018 from www.cnbc.com.

22 "Number of monthly active WeChat users from 3rd quarter 2011 to 3rd quarter 2018 (in millions)," retrieved 30 April 2018 from www.statista.com.

23 Eva Xiao (20 April 2017), "How WeChat Pay became Alipay's largest rival," retrieved 30 April 2018 from www. techinasia.com.

24 Joon Ian Wong and Johnny Simon (18 August 2017), "Photos: Inside one of the world's largest bitcoin mines," retrieved 24 May 2018 from https://qz.com.

25 Zheping Huang (5 January 2018), "This could be the beginning of the end of China's dominance in bitcoin mining," retrieved 24 May 2018 from https://qz.com; Wolfie Zhao (4 January 2018), "Report: PBoC quashes bitcoin mining ban rumor in China," retrieved 24 May 2018 from www.coindesk.com.

26 Helena Bedwell, Vanessa Dezem, Stephen Stapczynski and Jonathan Tirone (5 February 2018), "The cost of crypto is turning miners towards green power," retrieved 24 May 2018 from www.bloomberg.com.

27 Sara Hsu (15 January 2018), "China's shutdown of bitcoin miners isn't just about electricity," retrieved 24 May 2018 from www.forbes.com.

28 Zheping Huang (8 January 2018), "China wants an 'orderly exit' from bitcoin mining," retrieved 27 May 2018 from https://qz.com; Hsu, "China's shutdown of bitcoin miners isn't just about electricity."

29 Sidney Leng (5 February 2018), "Beijing bans bitcoin, but when did it all go wrong for cryptocurrencies in China?" retrieved 27 May 2018 from www.scmp.com.

30 Joseph Young (17 September 2017), "Japan Becomes Largest Bitcoin Market as Traders Leave China," retrieved 27 May 2018 from https://cointelegraph.com.

31 Emily Parker (11 December 2017), "Can China contain bitcoin?" retrieved 27 May 2018 from www.technologyreview.com.

32 Allen Scott (13 April 2018), "Russia's bitcoin mining industry takes root in Siberia," retrieved 27 May 2018 from http://bitcoinist.com.

33 "Bitcoin megacity could rise in Russia's Siberia," retrieved 28 May 2018 from www.rt.com.

34 Dieter Holger (25 February 2018), "Vladimir Putin endorses blockchain: Russia can't be 'late in the race'," retrieved 28 May 2018 from http://bitcoinist.com; "Vladimir Putin says Russia needs blockchain, cannot be late in the race", retrieved 28 May 2018 from www.ccn.com.

35 Samantha Chang (7 March 2018), "Russia to criminalize bitcoin use as money substitute: Putin to roll out laws,"

retrieved 28 May 2018 from www.investopedia.com; Holger, "Vladimir Putin endorses blockchain."

5. When It Hits the Fan

36 Stephen Gandel (23 July 2015), "Moody's, nearly seven years too late, admits miscalculation in subprime ratings," retrieved 31 May 2018 from www.fortune.com; Steve Denning (22 November 2011), "Lest we forget: Why we had a financial crisis," retrieved 31 May 2018 from www.forbes.com.

37 Gandel, "Moody's, nearly seven years too late, admits miscalculation in subprime ratings."

38 David Ellis (5 March 2009), "Citigroup breaks the buck," retrieved 8 June 2018 from http://money.cnn.com; "Citigroup American Company," (2001), in *Encyclopedia Britannica*, retrieved from Encyclopedia Britannica online; Jonathan Stempel (6 March 2009), "Citigroup stock falls below $1 for first time," retrieved 8 June 2018 from www.reuters.com.

39 "This Is How Much Money the World Owes," (18 April 2018), retrieved 14 June 2018 from http://fortune.com.

40 Daniel C.K. Chow, *China's Response to the Global Financial Crisis: Implications for U.S.–China Economic Relations*, 1 Global Bus. L. Rev. 47 (2010).

41 Dominic Frisby (14 May 2016), "Zimbabwe's trillion-dollar note: from worthless paper to hot investment," retrieved 20 June 2018 from www.theguardian.com.

42 Robert Brand, Brian Latham and Godfrey Marawanyika (15 November 2017), "Zimbabwe doesn't have its own currency and bitcoin is surging," retrieved 22 June 2018 from www.bloomberg.com; Shafi Musaddique (15 November 2017), "Zimbabweans turn to bitcoin as cryptocurrency value soars to $13,500," retrieved 22 June 2018 from www.independent.co.uk.

43 Will Martin (3 August 2017), "35% GDP collapse: Venezuela's unprecedented economic slide in numbers," retrieved 22 June 2018 from www.businessinsider.sg.

44 "Why are Venezuelans mining so much bitcoin?" (3 April 2018), retrieved 22 June 2018 from www.economist.com; Rene Chun (September 2017), "Big in Venezuela: Bitcoin mining," retrieved 22 June 2018 from www.theatlantic.com; John Otis (19 February 2018), "Venezuela's new bitcoin: an ingenious plan or worthless cryptocurrency?" retrieved 22 June 2018 from www.theguardian.com.

www.ingramcontent.com/pod-product-compliance
Lightning Source LLC
Chambersburg PA
CBHW020603220526
45463CB00006B/2429